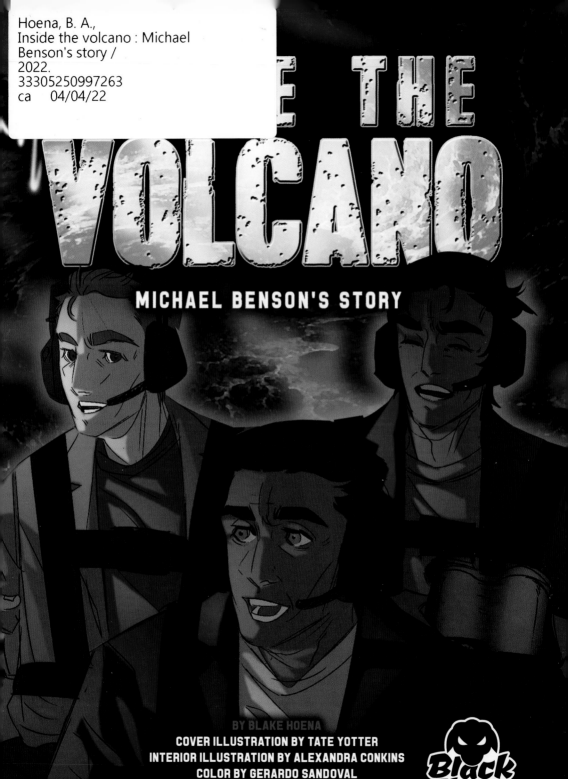

E THE VOLCANO

MICHAEL BENSON'S STORY

BY BLAKE HOENA

COVER ILLUSTRATION BY TATE YOTTER
INTERIOR ILLUSTRATION BY ALEXANDRA CONKINS
COLOR BY GERARDO SANDOVAL

Black Sheep

BELLWETHER MEDIA • MINNEAPOLIS, MN

STRAY FROM REGULAR READS
WITH BLACK SHEEP BOOKS.
FEEL A RUSH WITH EVERY READ!

This edition first published in 2022 by Bellwether Media, Inc.

No part of this publication may be reproduced in whole or in part without written permission of the publisher. For information regarding permission, write to Bellwether Media, Inc., Attention: Permissions Department, 6012 Blue Circle Drive, Minnetonka, MN 55343.

Library of Congress Cataloging-in-Publication Data

LC record for Inside the Volcano: Michael Benson's Story available at https://lccn.loc.gov/2021025034

Editor: Betsy Rathburn   Designer: Andrea Schneider

Printed in the United States of America, North Mankato, MN.

TABLE OF CONTENTS

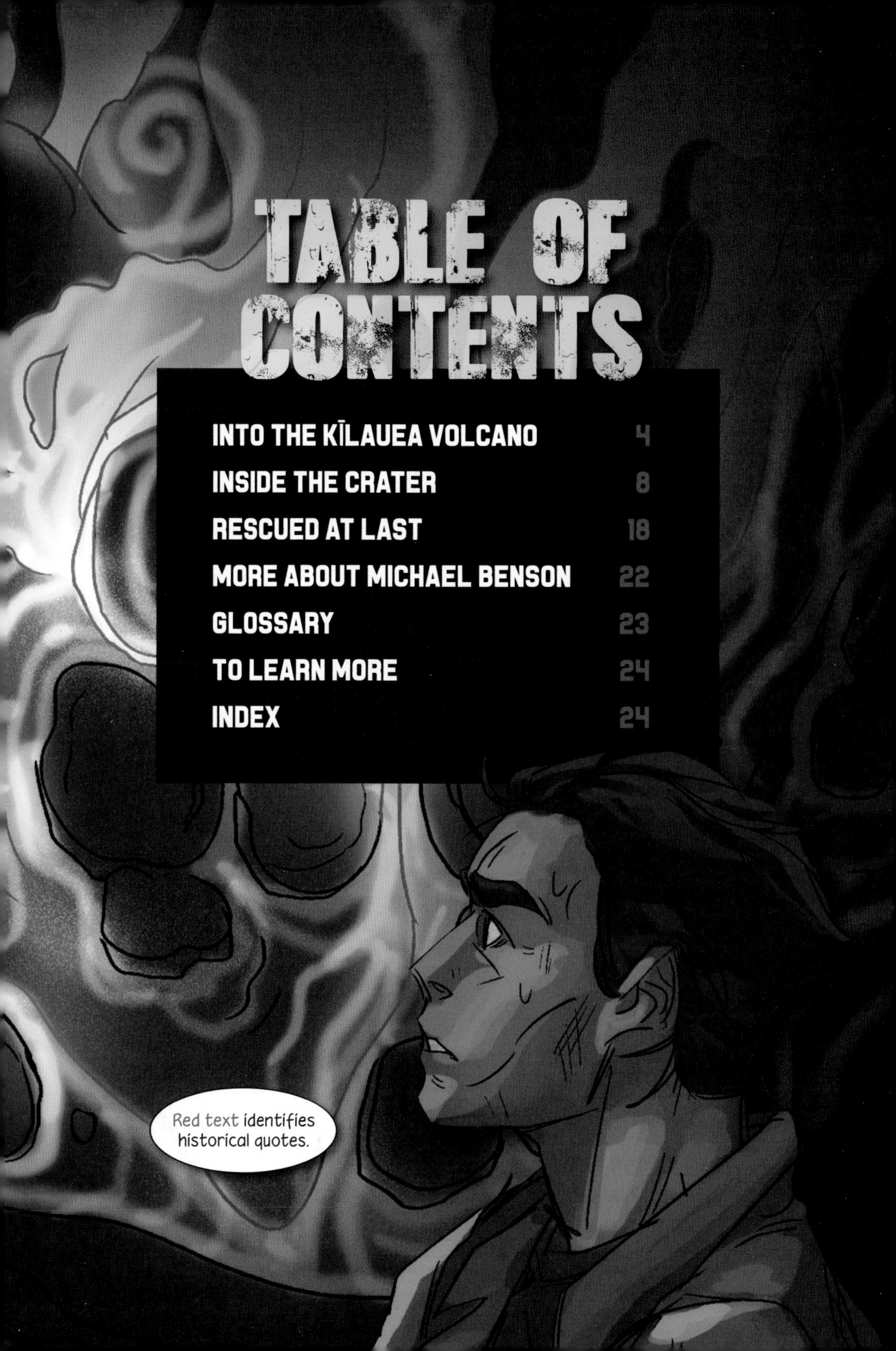

Red text identifies historical quotes.

INTO THE KĪLAUEA VOLCANO

It is November 21, 1992. A helicopter flies toward the Kīlauea volcano on the island of Hawaii. The pilot, Craig Hosking, is flying the helicopter. His passengers are cameraman Michael Benson and Michael's assistant, Chris Duddy.

They plan to fly over a part of Kīlauea known as the Puʻu ʻŌʻō **crater**. This crater has been erupting since the mid-1980s.

Michael is currently filming for a movie. For the movie's final scenes, he wants **footage** of the **lava** inside the Puʻu ʻŌʻō crater. But before flying over Kīlauea, there is something the crew of the helicopter must do.

Why are we doing this again?

It's an offering to Pele, to keep her happy.

And to keep us safe!

In Hawaiian **legends**, Pele is the **goddess** of volcanoes. It is **tradition** to offer her gifts in exchange for safety.

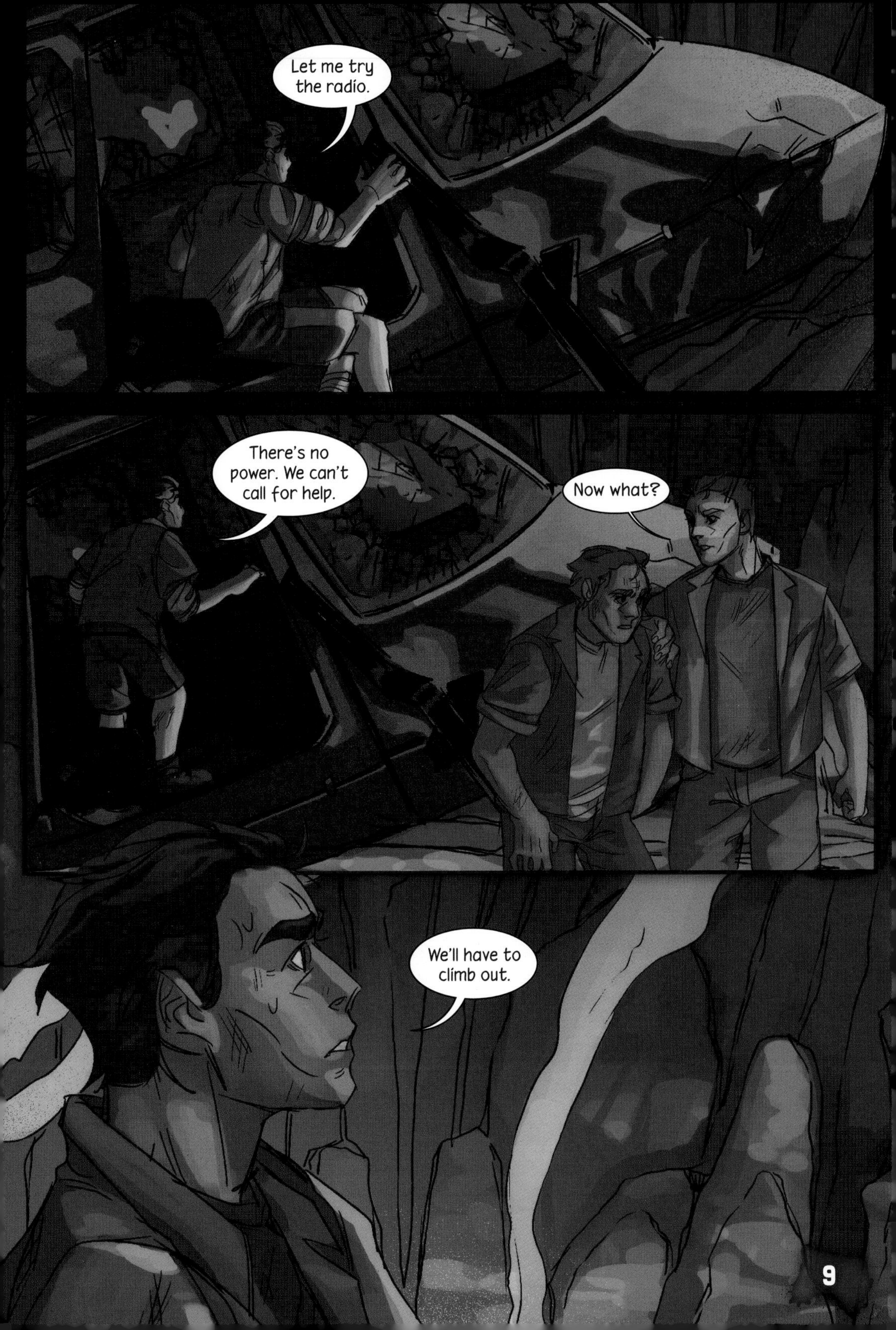
Let me try the radio.
There's no power. We can't call for help.
Now what?
We'll have to climb out.

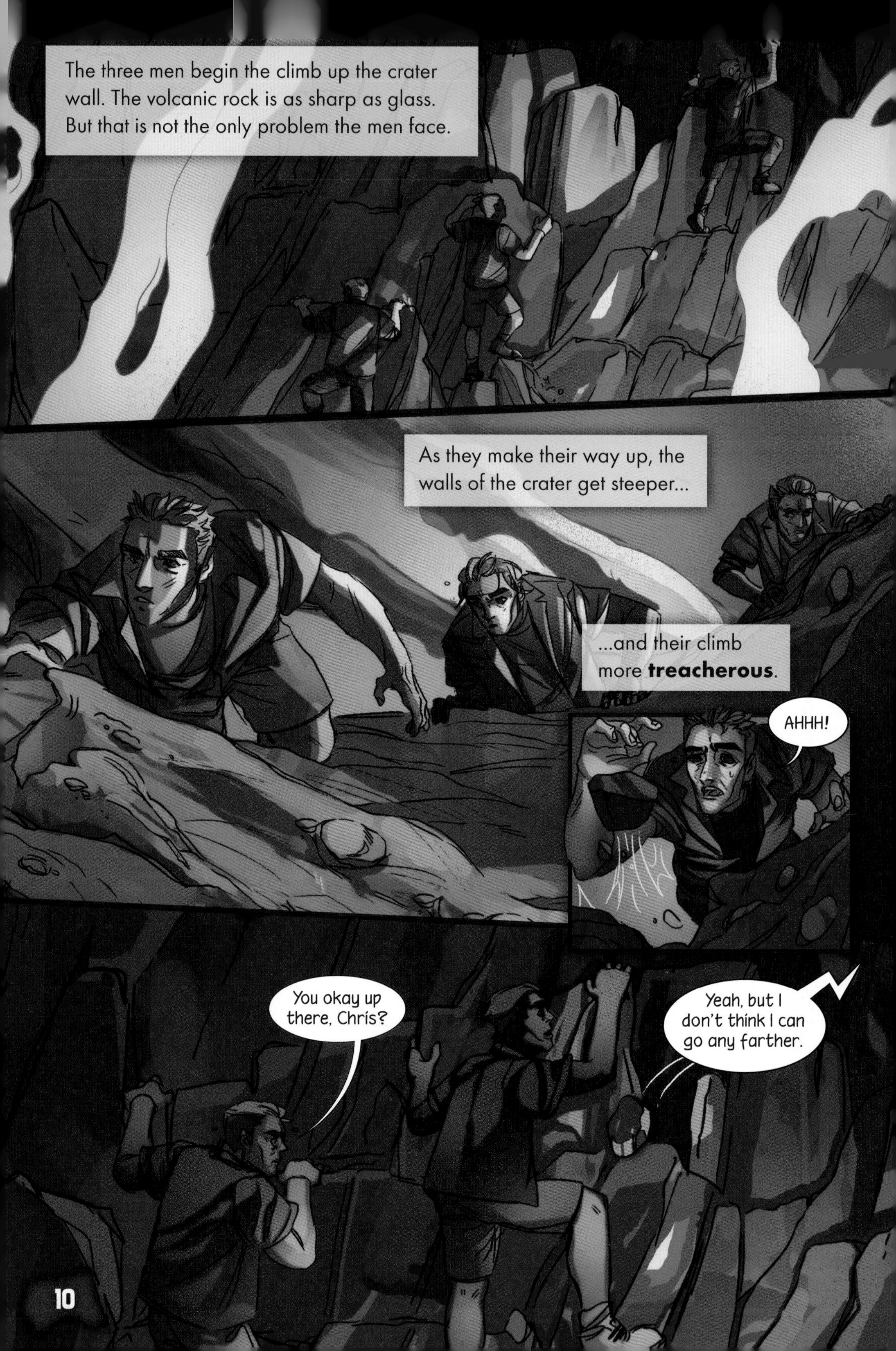

The three men begin the climb up the crater wall. The volcanic rock is as sharp as glass. But that is not the only problem the men face.
As they make their way up, the walls of the crater get steeper...
...and their climb more **treacherous**.
AHHH!
You okay up there, Chris?
Yeah, but I don't think I can go any farther.

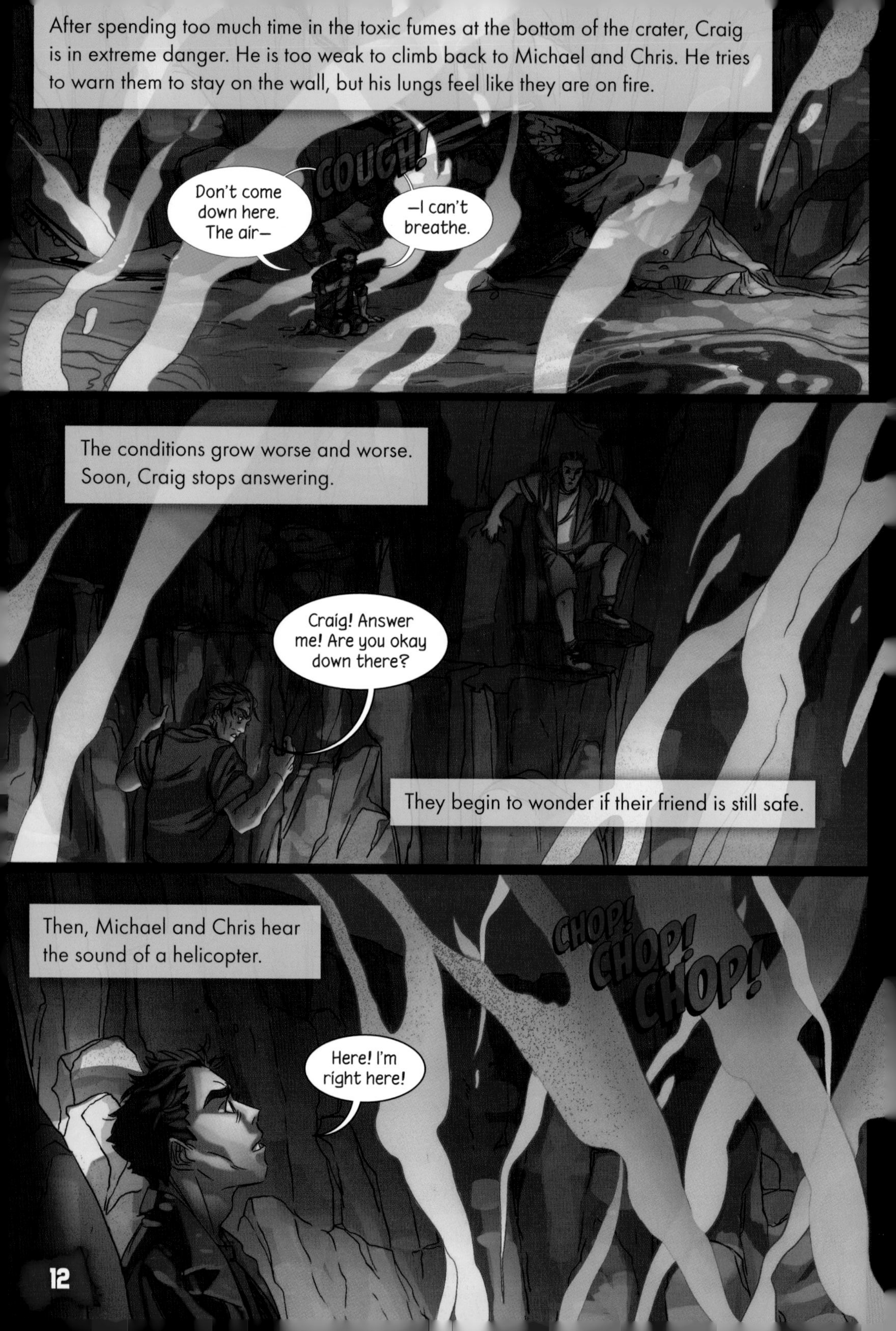
After spending too much time in the toxic fumes at the bottom of the crater, Craig is in extreme danger. He is too weak to climb back to Michael and Chris. He tries to warn them to stay on the wall, but his lungs feel like they are on fire.
Don't come down here. The air—
COUGH!
—I can't breathe.
The conditions grow worse and worse. Soon, Craig stops answering.
Craig! Answer me! Are you okay down there?
They begin to wonder if their friend is still safe.
Then, Michael and Chris hear the sound of a helicopter.
CHOP! CHOP! CHOP!
Here! I'm right here!

RESCUED AT LAST

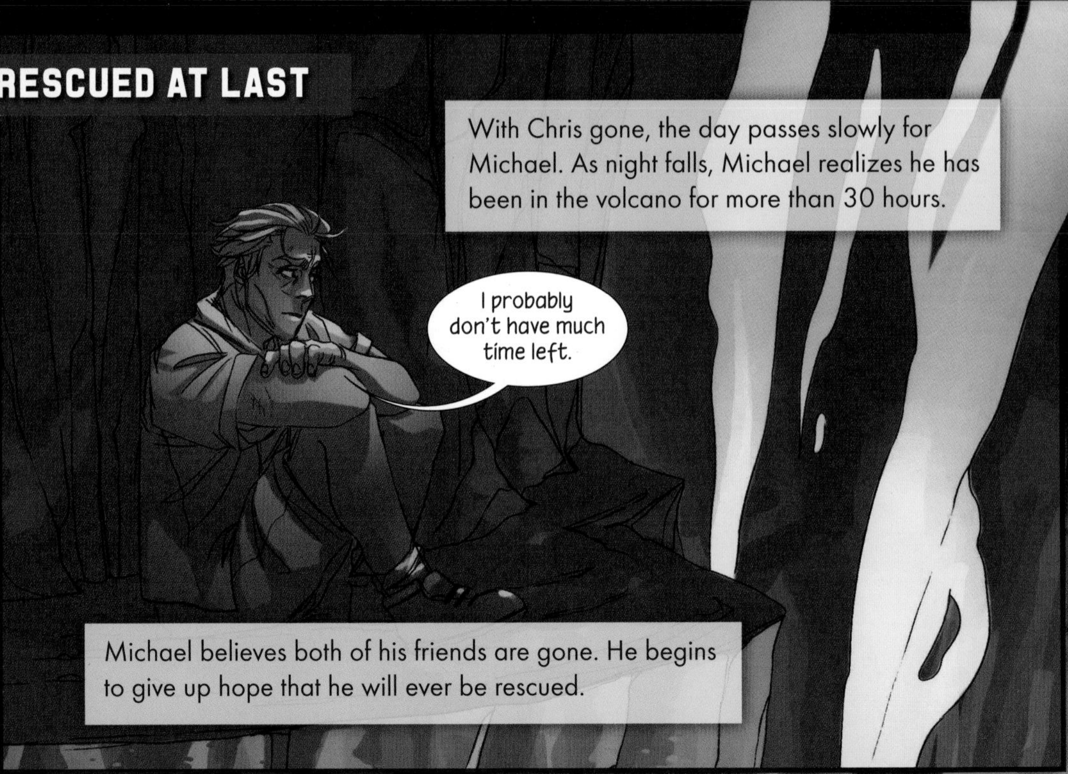
With Chris gone, the day passes slowly for Michael. As night falls, Michael realizes he has been in the volcano for more than 30 hours.
I probably don't have much time left.
Michael believes both of his friends are gone. He begins to give up hope that he will ever be rescued.

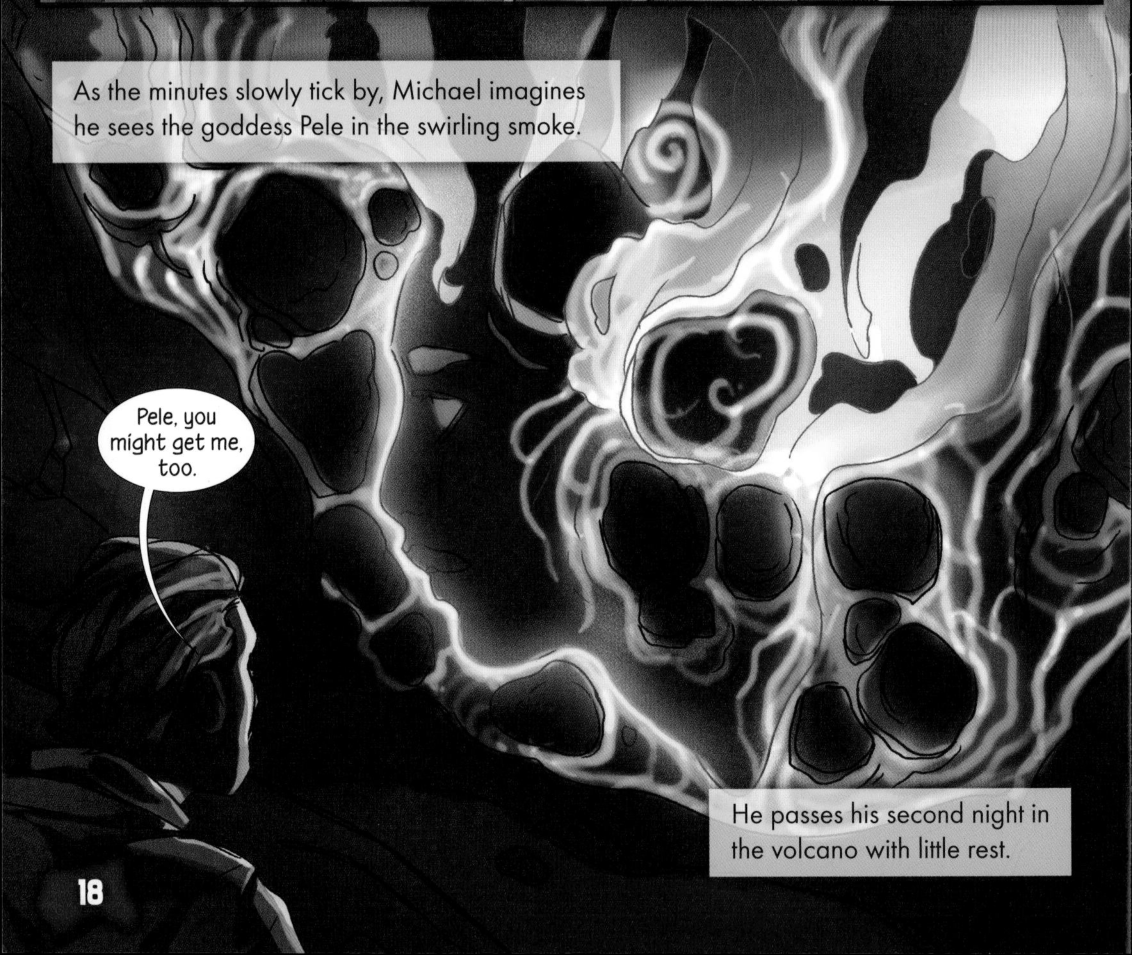
As the minutes slowly tick by, Michael imagines he sees the goddess Pele in the swirling smoke.
Pele, you might get me, too.
He passes his second night in the volcano with little rest.

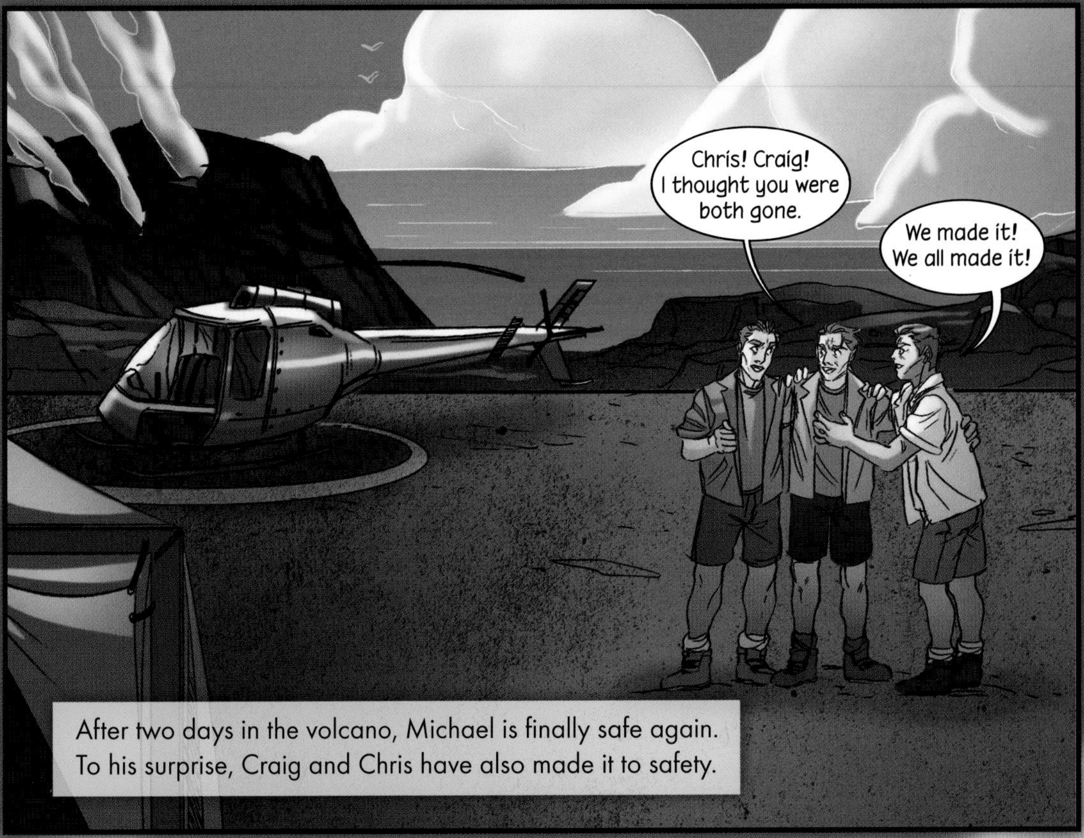
Chris! Craig! I thought you were both gone.
We made it! We all made it!
After two days in the volcano, Michael is finally safe again. To his surprise, Craig and Chris have also made it to safety.

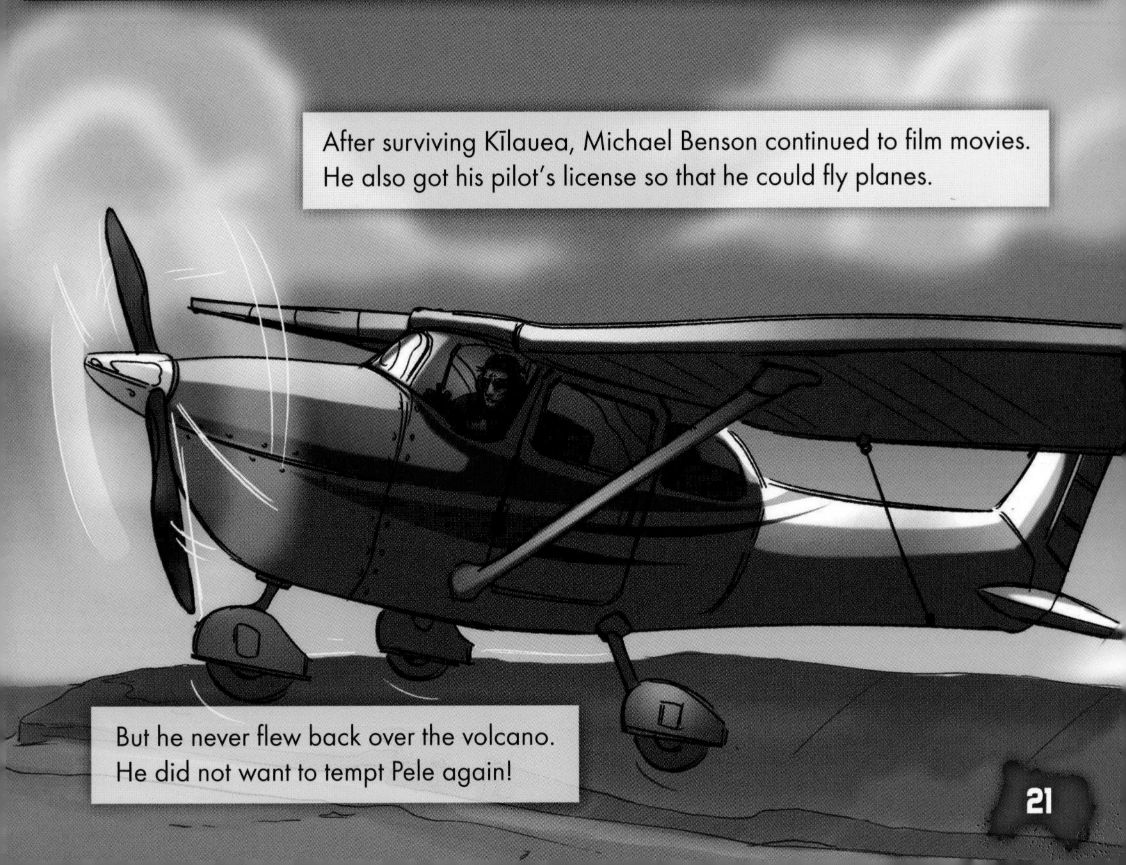
After surviving Kīlauea, Michael Benson continued to film movies. He also got his pilot's license so that he could fly planes.
But he never flew back over the volcano. He did not want to tempt Pele again!

MORE ABOUT MICHAEL BENSON

✚ The footage Michael filmed of the lava was destroyed in the crash.

✚ Michael has filmed dozens of Hollywood movies, including the 2000 movie *X-Men* and the 2006 movie *Mission: Impossible III*.

✚ After Craig fixed the radio battery, he was able to call for help. A helicopter pilot flew down into the crater to rescue him.

✚ Chris managed to climb out of the crater. Then he found an empty rescue camp. Water and oxygen at the camp kept him alive until he was rescued by a helicopter.

✚ After 35 years, the Puʻu ʻŌʻō crater stopped erupting in 2018.

MICHAEL BENSON TIMELINE

**morning of
November 21, 1992**
Michael Benson, Chris Duddy, and Craig Hosking crash-land into the Kīlauea volcano

November 22, 1992
Chris manages to climb out of the volcano

**afternoon of
November 21, 1992**
Craig is rescued by a helicopter

November 23, 1992
Michael is finally rescued by a helicopter

MICHAEL BENSON MAP

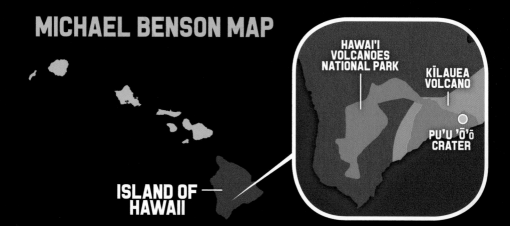

ISLAND OF HAWAII

HAWAI'I VOLCANOES NATIONAL PARK

KĪLAUEA VOLCANO

PUʻU ʻŌʻō CRATER

GLOSSARY

crater—a large hole in the ground

footage—film recorded for television or movies

fumes—smoke or gases that are dangerous to breathe in

goddess—a female god

lava—extremely hot, fluid-like rock

legends—old stories that are passed down over time

mayday—a call for emergency help

molten—liquified due to extreme heat

toxic—poisonous

tradition—a custom, idea, or belief handed down over time

treacherous—very dangerous

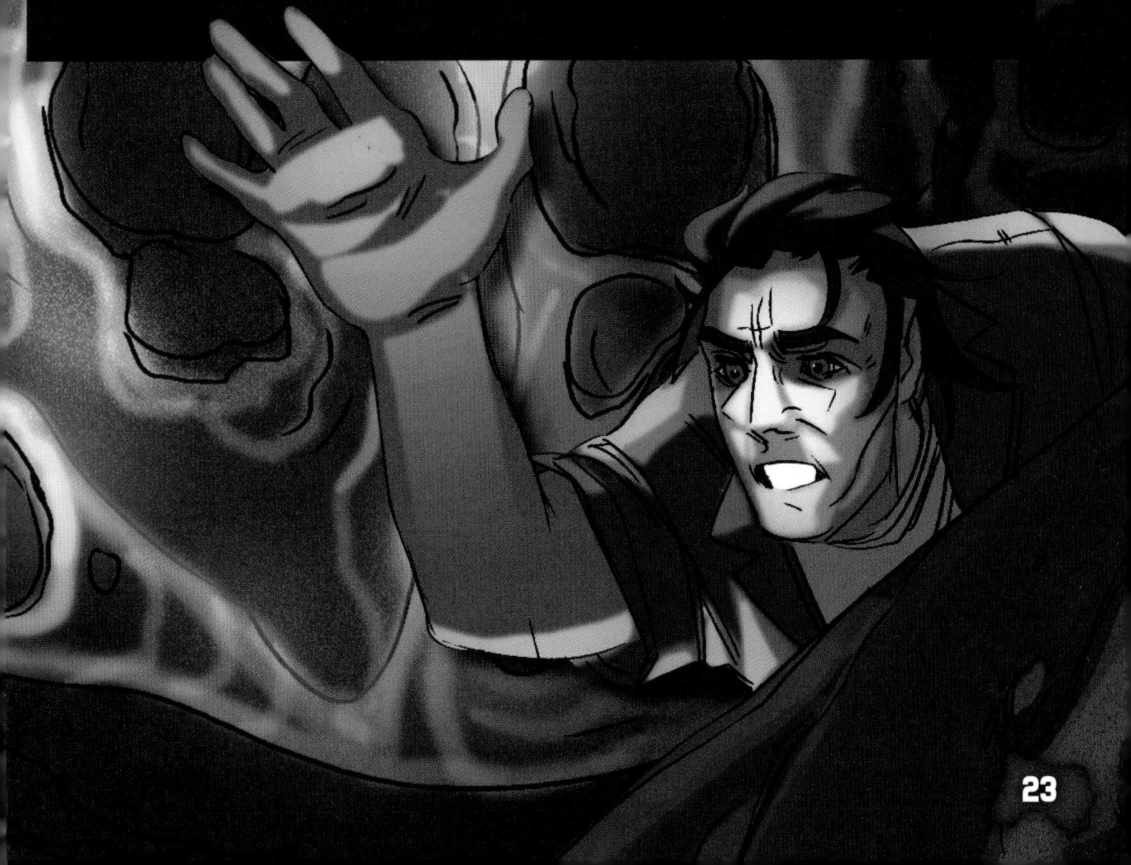

TO LEARN MORE

AT THE LIBRARY

Berg, Shannon. *Hawaii Volcano of 2018*. Lake Elmo, Minn.: Focus Readers, 2020.

Hamalainen, Karina. *Hawai'i Volcanoes*. New York, N.Y.: Children's Press, 2019.

Loh-Hagan, Virginia. *Michael Benson: Trapped in a Volcano*. Ann Arbor, Mich.: Cherry Lake Publishing, 2019.

ON THE WEB

FACTSURFER

Factsurfer.com gives you a safe, fun way to find more information.

1. Go to www.factsurfer.com
2. Enter "Michael Benson" into the search box and click 🔍.
3. Select your book cover to see a list of related content.

INDEX